presented to

from

date

UnCOMMON MANHOOD

SECRETS TO WHAT IT MEANS TO BE A MAN

TONY DUNGY

WITH NATHAN WHITAKER

TYNDALE

Tyndale House Publishers, Inc.
Carol Stream, Illinois

Visit Tyndale online at www.tyndale.com.

Visit the author's website at www.coachdungy.com.

TYNDALE and Tyndale's quill logo are registered trademarks of Tyndale House Publishers, Inc.

Uncommon Manhood: Secrets to What It Means to Be a Man
Copyright © 2012 by Tony Dungy. All rights reserved.

Published in association with the literary agency of Legacy, LLC, Winter Park, Florida 32789.

Literary development and design by Koechel Peterson & Associates, Inc., Minneapolis, Minnesota.

Unless otherwise indicated, all Scripture quotations are taken from the *Holy Bible*, New Living Translation, copyright © 1996, 2004, 2007 by Tyndale House Foundation. Used by permission of Tyndale House Publishers, Inc., Carol Stream, Illinois 60188. All rights reserved.

Scripture quotations marked NIV are taken from the Holy Bible, *New International Version*,® *NIV*.® Copyright © 1973, 1978, 1984, 2011 by Biblica, Inc.™ Used by permission of Zondervan. All rights reserved worldwide. www.zondervan.com. This book has been adapted from *Uncommon: Finding Your Path to Significance*, copyright © 2009 by Tony Dungy. Published by Tyndale House Publishers, Inc.

Printed in China

18   17   16   15   14   13   12
7   6   5   4   3   2   1

contents

COMMON MAN

what does it really mean to be a man?

The truth is that young men get pulled in every direction by people and society today. Everyone has a different expectation for us as men: be a provider, be tough, be sensitive, don't cry, go to work, stay home, go hang out with the boys, don't go hang out with the boys, and so on.

Over and over through the years, I've seen the results of these confusing messages. Unfortunately, the kind of ideas that our young men are buying into and the pressure to conform are causing them to follow the path of least resistance.

Things about manhood are accepted as normal without any thought as to whether they should be or whether there might be a better way. Too often we resign ourselves to accepting that things just are the way they are.

To all of that, I say this: being a man is more than leaving our wives husbandless, our children fatherless, our employers passionless, our families hopeless.

You can be more. You were created to be more—and better. The messages of the world are cop-outs; the messages of sexual conquest, of financial achievement, of victory in general. Not only are these messages not fair, but they also fall so short of what you can do—and more important, of who you can be.

In our journey to becoming men, we have to get back to the fundamentals, those basic principles that will allow us to succeed as men. We can be certain there will always be obstacles along the way. However, having those fundamentals to fall back on will help us overcome those obstacles. We are not only *able* to effect this change, but we *must.*

Often the path isn't clear and the keys to manhood aren't obvious. But at the end of the day, I'm sure of one thing: accumulating stuff and women and titles and money are wrong keys. Fitting in, following the crowd, and being common are not what we're supposed to do. There's more in store for us!

MY COLLEGE FOOTBALL COACH, CAL STOLL, OFTEN TOLD US,

"Success is UNCOMMON, therefore not to be enjoyed by the common man. I'm looking for uncommon people."

A TRUE MAN IS ONE WHO IS UNCOMMON.

In a common world, becoming an uncommon man begins by cultivating uncommon character.

UNCOMMON MANHOOD

{ develop
your core

{ Character **and its growth**

don't come from rules

but from the small actions

of responsibility

that occur day after day. }

character

What are the values that guide the decisions you make? Is the fact that you are moving up more important to you than *the way* you move up? Does it matter if you follow the rules or break them, just as long as you come out on top? Are you someone who says, "Since everyone is doing it, if I want to have a legitimate chance to compete, I have to do it too"?

I realize this is not necessarily the common approach today, but *what you do is not as important as how you do it.* Those are the words that keep coming back to me when I am tempted to choose what is expedient over what is right. People who bend the rules to get ahead usually get caught in the long run . . . and always know how they made it to the top as frauds.

The other problem is that, at some point, somebody who *does* care how the game is played—a boss, a board of directors—may find out. For me as an employer, *how you* do your job has always been more important than *what* you do. Can you be counted on to do things the right way, or will you cut corners and hope it turns out all right? Your character will determine the answer.

Character begins with the little things in life. We must show that we can be trusted with each and every thing, no matter how trivial it may seem. Over time, we create ourselves and build our character through the little acts we do.

Character is tested, revealed, and further *developed* by the decisions we make in the most challenging times. We have to know what is right, and we have to choose to do it. That is how character is developed—by facing those decisions and choosing the right way over and over until it becomes second nature. It's just how you do things.

Outwardly, character reflects an inner life committed to honor and uncompromising integrity.

My mom would say constantly,

"Your word is your bond."

That has become my standard for life. In the end, character is a blend of inner courage, wisdom, and a sense of duty to yourself, to others, and to something greater than you.

honesty
and integrity

As a boy, I thought my father coined the phrase *"The truth shall set you free."* He was actually quoting Jesus.

In our family, I quickly learned that skirting the rules will come back to hurt you. Whether it's doing something illegal or cheating on a test, you may get the edge and experience a short-term "win," but dishonesty will eventually catch up with you.

That's life. That's integrity. The choice between what's convenient and what's right. The lingering effect is that this choice carries longer-term consequences than we realize at the time.

Integrity is what you do when no one is watching; it's doing the right thing all the time, even when it may work to your disadvantage.

Integrity is keeping your word. It is that internal compass and rudder that directs you to where you know you should go when everything around you is pulling you in the opposite direction.

Integrity is critical to everything we do because it is the foundation of trustworthiness in our own eyes, in the eyes of those around us, and in God's eyes. Can I count on you as a teammate, as a business partner, or as a marriage partner? Can I count on you to do what you say you will do, no matter what difficulty may come along?

Our reputation is the public perception of our integrity. Because it is determined by other people's opinions of us, it may or may not be accurate, and it actually doesn't matter. It's important, but what others think of me is simply out of my control. What does matter, however, is what *I* think of me—my integrity. That is something I can control—by taking care of the little things, day in and day out, when no one is watching.

Because I am . . . and God is.

Integrity is no respecter of position or wealth or race or gender. It is not determined by shifting circumstances, cultural dynamics, or what you've previously achieved.

You alone determine whether you will be a person of *integrity.*

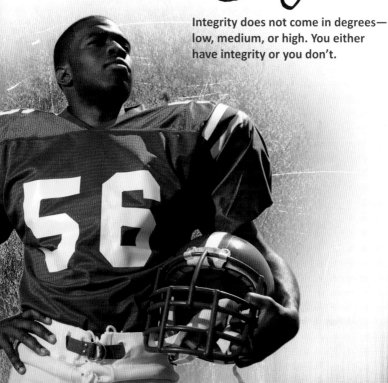

Integrity does not come in degrees—low, medium, or high. You either have integrity or you don't.

HUMILITY

{ Don't **blow your**

own horn. You are

important, but not

indispensable. }

humility and stewardship

Our society tells us that being flashy, loud, and proclaiming ourselves "the greatest" sells.

But "pride goes before destruction" (Proverbs 16:18). When someone crosses the fine line between confidence and pride, it results in fall after fall. Pride is all about me, but confidence is a realization that God has given me abilities and created me to fill a unique role that no one else is called to fill. Borne in humility, confidence is a recognition that life is not about me but about using the gifts and abilities I have been blessed with to their fullest to help my team, my coworkers, my family, and others.

To be humble is not false modesty, claiming that what you accomplished or who you are isn't important, but a realization that God created all of us with unique gifts and abilities. It's embracing the truth that God created you for a particular place and time and lifting others up who were also created to play a role. Once you can do that, it becomes much easier to let go of status or false ideas of respect.

Rather than insisting that others respect *us,* we need to make sure that we are respecting *others,* holding others in proper esteem. Those who live out this quality make the best spouses, teammates, parents, friends, and business partners.

In humility, when we realize that everything we have is a gift from God—our money, our time, our talents and abilities—we approach a clear understanding that the things we have in our control are His resources *entrusted* to us for wise usage, for *eternal* usage. When we see ourselves as the stewards or the trustees of the resources we control—not the owners—we are on the verge of understanding the true meaning of stewardship.

As stewards of all we have within our control, we must ask, Do I invest in eternity? Do I do things that will outlive me? Do I invest in the lives of others? Do I invest in the expansion of God's agenda?

Stewardship—it's all about God.

It is ordinary men—submitted and available to God—whom God uses to touch the lives of others.

He transforms the common work that we do into something majestic and eternal. Something UNCOMMON.

God needs only a gentle, pure, and humble life that is willing to be used in the simple, everyday moments of fathering, coaching, speaking, listening, sharing, and caring.

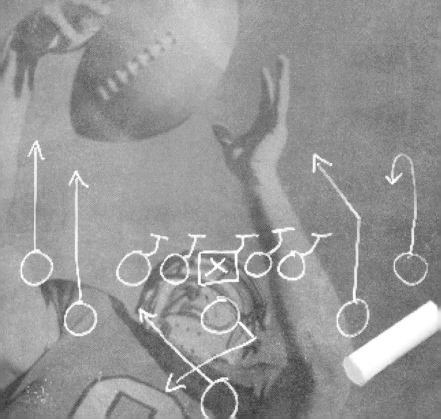

CO
URAGE

{ Some of the most rew

times in life are wher

have to stand alon

Never give up. Neve

courage

Being a man has never been easy. The demands on us are many. We get tugged, second-guessed, pulled in different directions, and at the end of the day we are often left wondering what happened.

One of the most important things I have learned along the way is having the courage to stand by my convictions—those things that I know are right, those guiding principles that I know to stick with. Sometimes that means standing out from the crowd or not being popular, but sometimes that's the only responsible place to be. It doesn't necessarily make the days any easier, but at least I feel like I'm still heading in the right direction.

No one is immune to peer pressure, and we're susceptible to it at any age. It's just that as we get older, we do a better job of rationalizing it or hiding it altogether. But through the years, I've learned another way of dealing with it. These days, when it comes to peer pressure, I make sure I know for myself what is right and am prepared to stick with it. Courage can be demonstrated by standing up to the school bully or intervening to prevent someone you don't know from being hurt. But more often than not, it's the day-to-day moments of reaching down inside yourself to find the courage to stand alone that can be the toughest.

I pay attention to my internal compass. I think it's always been there, guiding me, but as I've matured, I've listened to it better and more often. It helps me stay "lashed to the mast," as Homer wrote that Odysseus did to keep the Sirens from drawing him into destruction. That Greek myth resonates because we can relate to that feeling. Even when we know we are heading toward something that could lead to our destruction, it can still seem awfully appealing.

That internal compass, sharpened by having positive peers around me and by studying my Bible, keeps me lashed to the mast.

Martin Luther King Jr. was a man who stood by his convictions. Regardless of how he was being treated, he stood with dignity, grace, love, and courage.

Dr. King said,

"We will have to repent in this generation not merely for the hateful words and actions of bad people but for the appalling silence of the good people."

Stand by your convictions.
Summon the courage to be uncommon.

{ love your family

In a common world, to love as an uncommon man means doing everything, making every decision, with your family's well-being in mind.

{ Anything is possible if real love is at the heart of your relationship. }

how to treat a woman

Today's generation hasn't had the best teachers, because many of our dads either weren't around or somehow didn't show us how to truly love a woman. And TV and movies usually focus on erotic love, not emotional, spiritual love.

Many guys either demand respect from women or become completely passive around them. Neither is the right approach. According to 1 Corinthians 13, love means doing everything for her benefit. That doesn't mean giving in to her every wish or desire, but it does mean making every decision with her well-being in mind. It means honoring her with respect in every way.

The most important way to show love for your wife is to be involved: as a leader, listener, and encourager. Lead by helping with discipline, setting curfews and ground rules for the television and other technology use. Lead by being in unity with your wife. And just listen to her without trying to solve the problems of her day—so she knows you care. Tell her you love her, offer encouragement for something she's tried or wants to try, and hold her every time she comes close. Be there for her.

God brought us together in marriage to complement each other. We have each been given unique insights, passions, experiences, and wisdom—for the benefit of the relationship, for each other, and even for those beyond our immediate family. Love means to respect each other's gifts, abilities, wisdom, intuition, and insights and to allow for equal opportunity for input in decisions. It means you are willing to help in an area that is "her" responsibility in order to show your love and ensure her emotional well-being.

Our commitment to live up to the sacred vow we made with our wives is the difference between the common and the uncommon. Common knowledge today says that you show your wife love and respect until she fails to meet your expectations, then you move on to someone else who will. Christ, on the other hand, encourages the uncommon approach: "What God has joined together, let no one separate" (Matthew 19:6, NIV). We have a duty to make our marriages work, for better or worse. Be a man of your word, and love your wife as Christ loves His church.

God loves and values your wife—
just as she is, just as He created her—
and sent His Son to die for her.

An **UNCOMMON** man accepts all
of his wife—with all of her radiant
grace, beauty, and difference.

This truth has moved me to often pray for
forgiveness for all the times I've missed
enjoying the uniqueness of her creation—
her laughter, tenderness, acceptance—as
a result of my self-centeredness.

fatherhood

Contrary to common views on absentee fathers, your children need nurture from you as much as from their mother! It is *not* acceptable to not be part of your child's life as long as you meet your financial responsibilities.

Studies have shown that the father's relationship with his daughter will be the primary predictor in the success of her marriage, in her relationships with men, and in her sexual behavior prior to marriage. If her father fails to nurture, love, and make her feel secure, she will attempt to fill that void through relationships with other men. As for our sons, if there is no father to model proper behavior for them, they will never learn what it means to be a man or a father.

When it comes to being present—really *there* physically and emotionally in the lives of our children—the limitations and obstacles are enormous, especially if we are divorced, have long commutes, or constantly travel. But we have to sacrifice to make certain our children know they are precious.

Consider the words you speak to your children. "The tongue," the Bible says, "is a flame of fire" (James 3:6). Our words can uplift and heal and empower and delight and provide comfort—or not. Words can inspire, rekindle a sense of wonder, and provide direction, or they can dampen spirits, condemn ideas, and destroy initiative. Know that your children are always looking for affirmation that they matter—to *you*.

What we say as fathers is so important, but not nearly as much as what we do. Our children are watching and notice if we are living lives that are inconsistent with what we're saying and teaching. If you fail to demonstrate real love for your wife, your son or daughter will get the real message of what you believe. If they see that work and status are what drives you, they will learn what you really value.

Our children need to know that we're there to help them pick up the pieces of their shattered dreams, to tell them they're okay, to help them see that failure isn't final, and that when they take their next steps, they will not be alone.

Listen to the gentle whisper from a God who daily reminds us to enjoy the sacred moments we have with our children.

The day will come when the playroom will be neat, tidy, and in perfect order, noticeably devoid of the laughing and chattering personalities of God's little angels in our home.

Fill your home with wonderful memories rather than regrets. See the fingerprints of God from His precious little messengers rather than a memorial of might-have-beens.

respect
authority

As I was growing up, my parents made it very clear that I was to honor them as the Bible commanded, through my obedience and respect (Exodus 20:12). I could disagree with them, and often did, but I had to accept their decisions and learn to deal with them patiently. As I got older, it became increasingly clear that my best interests were paramount to my parents.

Our parents aren't the only source of authority in our lives, however. In Romans 13:1-2, the apostle Paul told the early church in Rome that they must obey even the Roman rulers. Certainly there are exceptions to this scriptural admonition when authorities abuse their power. But let this principle guide you when what you are being asked to do isn't illegal or immoral or contrary to your loyalty, relationship, or allegiance to God.

I realize that you may have a hard time with this whole idea of honoring your parents and respecting authority. Many bear scars of abuse—physical, emotional, or otherwise—and broken homes. Perhaps you feel that you have the right to be angry for what was done to you, and you don't want to let it go. You may even feel that what you experienced was somehow your fault, and the hurtful actions of others have colored your view of our heavenly Father.

You don't want that to be the story for the rest of your life! You may need to seek professional help or talk to a pastor or trusted friend. But somehow you need to get to a place of healing and wholeness and move on into all the fullness of life that God intended for you to live. Unresolved bitterness ties us down and holds us back from becoming all we were created to be. You need to forgive the people who hurt you.

Whether you realize it or not, God created you with unique gifts and abilities, and He has given you a unique purpose. He wants to use you for extraordinary accomplishments. God wants you to experience His unconditional and never-ending love, the kind of love you may not have experienced from your parents. He wants to bless you with a sense of affirmation and wholeness in your life. He might even help you get to the place with your parents— either in person or in your heart—where you can not only let go of the pain but also honor them by giving them the blessing of your love.

God stands ready to walk with you
for the rest of your life.

The God who created you will never leave you and will always love you.

He will help you draw a line
between your past and your future,
and He will help you to forgive and
to move into all the fullness and
freedom of a brand-new day.

UN
COMMON
MAN-
HOOD

{ lift your
friends
and others

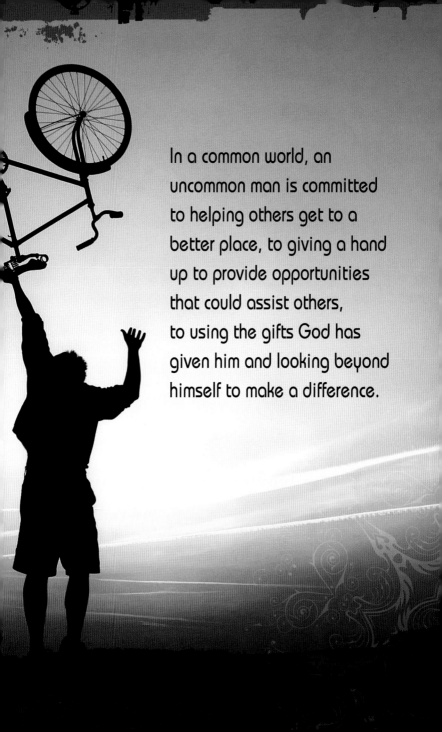

In a common world, an
uncommon man is committed
to helping others get to a
better place, to giving a hand
up to provide opportunities
that could assist others,
to using the gifts God has
given him and looking beyond
himself to make a difference.

FRIENDSHIP

{ Choose your friends for the

sake of friendship. }

friendship

Don't choose friends because they are popular, good-looking, rich, or athletic. Choose your friends because you enjoy them and because they are good people. Keep in mind that friendship runs two ways. Too often we evaluate a friendship based on the way it benefits us. But lasting friendships are formed when we can cause some benefits to flow toward someone else.

And choose your friends based on their values, not their status in society. My parents encouraged me to hang around people who had inner cores that would build me up. Friends who have and will reinforce the values ingrained in me when I am with them. At the same time, my parents discouraged me from hanging around people who didn't share our values. I knew I should be friendly to them, but I shouldn't befriend them. Look for people of character whose company you enjoy.

Within your circle of friends are the ones you seek out when you make your most important decisions. Those whose voices and wisdom you seek when you face a crossroads in your life. Friends who will stand by and guide as well as correct and admonish you when you need it. Friends who put your interests before their own. Friends who see the same direction for your life that you see—God's direction.

Too many of us listen to the voices of the crowd that are the loudest—voices of ambition, power, wealth, revenge, greed, pleasure, self-centeredness, and appeasement:

"Go ahead; no one will find out."

"Who can it hurt?"

"Your job is at stake; you'd better do it."

"Compared to what others are doing, this is nothing."

But even while these messages bombard us, we need to listen to the quiet voices consistently speaking the truth. These voices come from our wives and parents or close friends, those people who have been with us in the valleys and on the mountaintops of our journeys.

If we listen closely,
we may even hear

the quiet voice,
**the whisper of our God,
our dearest friend,**

pointing us toward the
UNCOMMON life
that He desires from us.

take counsel

There will always be someone who knows more than you do and from whose knowledge you can benefit. Being open to learning—to being mentored—is necessary for growth, but it is difficult for some to master. Too often, ego or pride has a way of hindering our growth and development.

Don't be someone who acts as if no idea is a good idea unless it's *his* idea. Be open to taking counsel. After all, Proverbs tells us that "plans succeed through good counsel; don't go to war [or to work!] without wise advice" (Proverbs 20:18).

A good coaching staff, for instance, is made up of people who are willing to listen to others. If I had all the answers as the head coach, there would be no point in hiring assistant coaches. The truth is, however, that we all need to surround ourselves with the very best, smartest, and most trustworthy people we can find and empower them to do their jobs. Let them know how significant their differing skills and abilities are to the mission of the cause, team, or organization, and allow them to use those gifts to get you there. Seek their input, listen to them, decide on the direction, and go there together.

Don't relish conflict, but don't fear it. Conflict is best seen as an opportunity to understand our differences. When a problem comes up, think constructively. You are not attacking the other person, and hopefully he is not attacking you, either. If he is, redirect him to the problem and focus on it.

It is common for people to let arguments become personal—name-calling, mockery, personal attacks. Failing to stay focused on the problem, we get frustrated and lash out, or we realize that our position should change, but we aren't confident enough to do so.

Don't be like that. Be constructive. Be uncommon. Stay focused on solutions and communication. Admit when you're wrong, but stand your ground when you're right . . . even if you're all alone. Either way, conflict can serve to illuminate truth or illuminate differences. In any event, it doesn't have to be feared.

When you are seeking counsel,
you are looking for someone who
is already ahead of you, someone
you can learn from.

Surround yourself

with the best people you can find,
seek their input, listen to them, and
become the best you can be.

It could very well make the difference
between common and uncommon results.

the power
of influence

Shakespeare's words "To thine own self be true" are no less true today for young men than they were four centuries ago and are critically important to remember as you set out in the world. You will come into contact with people who, whether they mean to or not, will exert pressure on you to conform. However, you are also in a position to influence them—for good. You can help your friends make better decisions just by your example. But to be a good example, you must have a clear foundation of who you are.

You were created for a purpose. It doesn't matter what you missed in the past or how you may have messed up; the fact is that your future is still ahead of you. What will you do with it? What did you learn from past mistakes that might make the journey ahead better? And which of those lessons do you need to model for those around you? Each day we are faced with challenges and the temptation to conform. But God made each of us with unique gifts and characteristics, and being a positive role model starts with being ourselves.

Be yourself—the self that God created!

Remember that it's in real-life, face-to-face connections that the power of our personal influence can have life-changing, long-lasting impact. My concern is that in today's forming of virtual bonds, we may be forsaking true human interaction and losing opportunities to build the most meaningful relationships. Connect with the people directly in front of you without all the distractions of modern technology.

Do you want to have a positive influence on the life of someone else? Visit or call or write someone whom you know is in need of encouragement. Take your wife out on a date or take a "date night" with your little girl. Send flowers to someone for no particular reason.

No matter where you are in your life's journey, you can begin today to be very intentional about leaving a trail of positive memories in the lives of those around you. Memories they will cling to in the rough spots they face in life. Memories that will draw them closer to you and affirm their value to you and to themselves. Why not start now?

Becoming a positive role model,
a person of influence,
starts with a look in the mirror.

**You have the power of influence to
do something that will forever be a
positive memory in someone's life.**

*Why not create a few fond and
unforgettably good memories
along the way for people you love?*

MENTORING

{ Be intentional about helping others as you move through life. }

mentoring

Aristotle noted, "We cannot learn without pain," and without the negative feedback of pain that God allows in our lives, we would miss many of life's most important lessons.

Many of these lessons we'd rather not learn at all. I'd rather be able to pass on to my children the things that I've learned the hard way, allowing them to skip over those painful experiences altogether. But some lessons won't register without the actual pain.

Or on the flip side, in discussing his scientific accomplishments, Isaac Newton wrote, "If I have seen further, it is by standing upon the shoulders of giants." Whether those giants are parents teaching their children or friends and family who have proved that their counsel can be trusted, Newton was referring to those people who look out for our best interests and help us become all we were intended to be. True giants have proved that they are wise, experienced, and loyal—strong enough to hold us on their shoulders.

Derrick Brooks and Warrick Dunn are two professional athletes who are leaving an amazing legacy through their mentoring. For many years, Brooks has worked with the Boys & Girls Clubs, and Dunn has helped single mothers purchase homes. They are reaching back to help others get to a better place, giving a hand up to provide opportunities that assist others, to use the gifts that God has given them and look beyond themselves to make a difference.

Not everyone has the financial means of an NFL player, but that's not the most important part of mentoring. It's about the time and sacrifice one gives. Teachers do this every day, for example. Most teachers could pursue other vocations that pay more and cause less stress, but they sacrifice in order to build into the lives of young people. They choose to mentor, to leave a legacy.

Look outside of yourself for someone you can reach out to. You don't have to be an NFL head coach to do it. My most satisfying interactions have been with young men who didn't know what I did for a living. They only knew that I was willing to stop, listen, care, and help.

The same is true for you, too.

At its essence, mentoring is building
character into the lives of others and
leaving a legacy.

*Trust me; there is a child out there
who needs to know that you care.*

In a common world, an uncommon man focuses
on fulfilling all that he was designed to be,
even when it involves the road less traveled.

{ your full
potential

POWERFUL

{ Build high expectations into

yourself and others. }

powerful thoughts

Our minds are powerful instruments. We have an amazing ability to accomplish whatever our minds tell us we can do. The great American psychologist and philosopher William James directed, "Be not afraid of life. Believe that life is worth living, and your belief will help create the fact." James sounds like a football coach who's trying to turn a losing team into a winning one. The first thing you have to do is create the belief that the team can win. Often the talent is already there, but there is no belief that winning will happen.

Being disciplined in your approach to each day of your life and accomplishing the things you dream of starts by disciplining your thoughts. Focus on the thoughts you *want* to occur, not those that you do *not* want to occur. Whatever we tend to think will often be the outcome of any given situation. I've seen the law of "self-fulfilling prophecies" carried out on athletic fields and people's lives over and over.

Building expectations is something we all have to do. When I started as an NFL assistant coach in 1981, there were no African American head coaches or coordinators—none. On day one, I didn't declare I was going to be a head coach or win a Super Bowl, but I believed that if I learned all I could learn and did my job well, I'd get promoted. If I became good enough, it would just be a matter of getting the opportunity.

That part I couldn't control, so I had to leave the opportunity in God's hands. But I never once allowed myself to believe that I couldn't do the job if I got the chance. And over the next fifteen years, even when I wasn't sure I would ever get that chance, I had to keep negativity out of my thought process and leave it with God.

You won't always rise to the level of the expectations you have for yourself, but you will never be able to rise above the imaginary ceiling you construct in your mind. How high do you want to set your expectations? How high would you like to go? Allow your mind and heart to embrace that direction.

Writing about the power of the tongue,
New Testament author James notes that both fresh
and salt water cannot flow from the same spring,
or as my friend Ken Whitten says,

"What's down in the well will come up in the bucket."

What is down in your well?
From what source do you draw
strength and direction for your life?
Whatever is there will govern the thoughts
for your today and tomorrows.
Fill it well.

education
and athletics

Two student athletes I knew when I went to the University of Minnesota, Ernest Cook and Charles Sims, had the opportunity to become professional athletes but chose not to because they were first focused on their careers. They went against the peer pressure and took an uncommon route through the adventure of life. Their example inspired me to do well in school academically.

Today's peer pressure within our society toward athletic achievement is extreme. We see it when children are pushed to compete in sports. We see it in the overzealous Little League parents and sometimes coaches who have lost all touch with reality. The kids are being pushed and coached like adults, with the idea that they have to be the best players on their teams so they can go to "the next level."

In the meantime, those children are often not encouraged to spend the same time and attention obtaining a full and complete education, even though they will need to use their education in their lives far more than their athletic training. And the same is true for those who make it into the professional ranks: post-career skills are crucial.

The other side effect of this focus on athletic achievement is that the true meaning has often been lost, submerged in a society that idolizes sports. Sports should be about enjoyment, cooperation, team building, learning to deal with adversity, building character, and pursuing excellence. Many kids today don't even get to have fun with their youth sports. I hear too many stories of eight-year-olds who have given up other sports because one coach thinks they should pursue a single sport *year-round,* including *traveling teams*. At eight years old? On the off chance that the child might be that one in a million to play a major league sport or be in the Olympics?

My parents supported my involvement in sports and other activities, but they wanted me to be well-rounded. As for me, I had the opportunity to play professional sports, but my career was over by the age of twenty-five, and I've needed other life skills to support myself. We need to give children a chance to explore and develop. Life is an adventure, and they need to be stretched beyond those activities at which they excel.

Keep the role of sports in your life in perspective. Enjoy yourself and love the competition.

The cold, hard facts are that something like one-tenth of one percent of high school athletes will become professional athletes.

Make sure you do everything in your power to fulfill all that you were designed to be. Oh, that you would not live your whole life with your talents untapped!

career, work, and money

What am I doing with my life? We all need to answer the deep questions of purpose, meaning, and fulfillment.

But don't be paralyzed over your career choice. You might not find the career path that gets you excited right away. Keep looking, but give your current position a chance. Many positions aren't terribly exciting, but they may be important stepping-stones to subsequent ones, and employers often are evaluating employees' abilities, commitment, and trust level. On the other hand, don't get stuck in a position you don't like. If you passively wait for life to come to you, you might be waiting a while.

It's great to love your work, and a blessing to enjoy it. Rather than making career choices on the basis of money, select something *that you want to do*. Money may get you started, but it won't be enough to sustain you when the times become difficult. It's always tempting to think that earning more money makes you a better provider for your family or means your employer values you more. The reality is, however, money isn't a good measure of what's best for you or your family. In fact, the more you base critical decisions on monetary evidence, the more your children will come to believe that money is the most important thing in your life . . . and ultimately, in theirs.

Having said that, keep in mind that poor money decisions can tie your hands, reduce your options, and cause you to make bad decisions out of desperation. Spending beyond your means and borrowing money is expensive—just look at credit card interest rates—and may limit the career choices you have down the road. Don't go there.

Many of us need to learn to let go of the day's frustrations when we go home. Whether it's your family or friends—or your blood pressure—no one deserves to be saddled with whatever happened at the workplace, so make a conscious decision to disengage from its trials and troubles. Tomorrow will have enough problems of its own. Don't let the emotion of the day govern your home life and free time negatively.

When you've given a solid day's work,
let your work stand for what it is.
And when you get home, be home.

Make sure that you're not so busy making a living that you forget to actually live.

Your friends, your wife, your children—
and even you yourself—
deserve quality, fully committed time.

Live! Now!

GOALS AND RIS

{ Don't fear risk—

life is an adventure,

not a dress rehearsal. }

goals and risk

Without goals in life—your own goals, not someone else's—you won't reach all that you're capable of becoming. Unless you are focused on the passions of your heart and are striving toward them, you won't achieve all that God has in store for you.

My goals were usually qualitative rather than quantitative. I never aimed for a particular number of games to win, but rather for a team that was as good as it could be and guys who were an asset to the community and good role models. I measured our teams by how we performed compared to our potential—that's really the only reasonable measurement to use.

As for me, I focus on goals that are within my control. My goal as I worked my way up to a head coach was to learn and improve so that I might merit consideration for the next step up. But I couldn't control whether or not I advanced. Some things are up to others—and God—and therefore aren't realistic to hold over yourself.

Sometimes those goals require risk. The old saying that "you can't steal second with your foot still on first" is true not only in baseball but also in life. There really is no safe path through life. We need to gather as much information as possible at the time, pray about things, make a decision, and move on.

Certainly, I learn from my decisions and the consequences so I don't repeat mistakes in the future, but I don't second-guess choices I've already made. It isn't productive. Unless you get a chance to undo those decisions, it's best to press on and give yourself a break, while doing the best you can with where you are.

Sometimes others will second-guess your decisions, especially if they don't share your view of the world. Many people believe that you should never pass up advancement at work—and the resulting money and status. If you pass up promotion—or quit a position—because of its impact on your family, the critics will suggest you're being irresponsible.

Don't listen to them. Have the courage of your convictions. Be uncommon.

Some of your decisions will pan out;
some will be disasters.

**One great life lesson I've learned
is that no one wins every game.
And we can win championships
even after losing some games.**

Either way, we've won in my book,
because we stepped out of the illusion of security
and are fully active in the game of life.

alcohol and drugs

Just because drinking alcohol isn't the right choice for me doesn't mean that others can't partake; after all, Jesus' first miracle was turning water into wine. And I'm not opposed to parties—Jesus went to plenty of parties.

What I do mind is our society's inability to see alcohol for what it is: a drug. We strongly warn against tobacco and illegal drugs but seem to look the other way with alcohol and set a disturbing example for our young people. While I agree it's right to not allow anyone to drink who is under the age of twenty-one, the fact that it's forbidden seems to have made drinking more attractive as well as made the twenty-first birthday drink a rite of passage into manhood.

Based upon my profession in the NFL and the fact that the league derives a great deal of revenue from alcohol sponsorships, which helps to pay my salary, I've struggled often with this issue. I know that my work indirectly promotes alcohol consumption on dangerous levels. Personally, I would be willing to live with less money if it would keep even one kid from making a mistake.

My father's choice to not drink any alcohol was a powerful example for me. My respect for my dad helped me make the same choice with confidence when the opportunity came my way. In addition, I also benefited from positive peer pressure when I noticed some of the other Steelers players giving beers back to the attendants on the flight home after my first road game. It brought home the truth of Romans 14:21: "It is better not to eat meat or drink wine or do anything else if it might cause another believer to stumble." Their example helped me not to stumble.

As for any other mind-altering substances, my advice is simple: just don't bother. The upside is so limited and fleeting, but the downside, coming either from one bad decision or a lifetime of addiction struggles, is not worth it. Every day, young people die tragically as a result of alcohol and drug abuse. It simply cannot be worth the risk.

Be careful with alcohol, and don't get near anything else that's mind-altering.

How do you know you'll be able to remain in control and "drink responsibly"?
How can you be certain you won't become addicted?

It's just not worth being part of the crowd in that way, and the downside may be far worse than the upside could ever be.

{ **True toughness** is how

you respond to **adversity.** }

FAILURE

failure

I'm often introduced today as one of only three people to win a Super Bowl as a player and as a head coach. What they don't always say is that there were twenty-seven straight seasons that ended in disappointment between those two Super Bowl wins.

The beauty of what I've learned through a life of sports, however, is that failure happens—regularly. And failure, as it turns out, is a constant human experience. I've also learned that if you're afraid of failure, you won't try to do very much. But if you're going to chase meaningful dreams and do significant things, you have to be willing to come up short sometimes. Count on it. The more I learned about those people I admired for their successes, the more I also admired them for the way they handled failures.

People rarely want to discuss their own failures. But in reality, we're all wearing masks to cover our shortcomings, all thinking that feelings of self-doubt and misgiving are ours alone. Nothing could be further from the truth; failure is part of being human.

To truly accomplish your goals and improve involves a journey through adversity and failure. Adversity makes us stop and evaluate how we could have done something better to become successful. In weight lifting, muscle fibers are broken down when they are stressed, which leads to muscle growth. The same is true for other kinds of growth.

Toughness is shown in how you respond to adversity. Can you respond without losing your footing and your direction? If so, that shows me you're tough. The truly tough man is the one who stays grounded in his values and focused on his goals when things in life don't go according to plan. He exhibits a determination to reach his goal no matter the obstacles.

Whatever comes your way, know that God is constantly working in you through it all, molding and shaping you into who He created you to be.

Through pressure, stress, and adversity, we are strengthened—in our character, in our faith, and in our ability to give it one more try.

Success
is really a journey of persistence and perseverance in spite of failure.

It's in the valley of our failures where God is working the hardest, making us into something uncommon.

{ establish a mission that matters

In a common world that emphasizes style and what a man does, an uncommon man realizes that substance and who a man is are what really matter.

SUBSTANCE

{ Be aware that the world

emphasizes style, but substance

is what really matters. }

style versus substance

There are a lot of perceptions today about manhood, masculinity, and how to succeed in this world. I think we have to look deeper into things and use resources such as the Bible to help us define what manhood truly is. Some of the definitions that our young men are living by today don't give them a chance to succeed.

One of the most compelling and distorted perceptions is that respect comes from status. We tend to focus on what we do, how much we earn, what we look like, what we wear, and what we have. Therefore, it becomes important to us to have a job that will provide the type of status we want, as well as enough income to be able to buy the stuff that will add that status. The media equates all these things with a certain level of respect, which gets played up in magazines, television shows, and movies. Such a constant onslaught perpetuates the idea that respect comes from status.

And then, all too often, we begin to view and evaluate other people by these standards. If they don't measure up, we decide they probably aren't successful and don't have significance, and therefore we don't respect them.

With this mind-set, status becomes one of the most important measures of a man's masculinity. It's style over substance, perception over reality—everywhere you look. Success, or at least the appearance of success, becomes more important than anything else. Anything that diminishes that appearance also touches on the man's feeling of significance and worth.

The real danger is that choosing style over substance keeps us from valuing those things that truly have worth. Being a good parent, being a loyal and committed husband, modeling proper behavior for others, mentoring the less fortunate—these things may not give us status in today's world, but they are important to God.

Substance or style—the choice is clear if we want to live the significant lives we were meant to live.

A good first step in developing a solid game plan for becoming an uncommon man is to know exactly who you are—or should be—beyond the perceptions of the world.

Manhood is not about the car you drive or the clothes you wear.

Somewhere we've lost the concept that respect comes from appreciating who a person is inside and what he is truly all about. We don't respect the man; we respect what he does and what he has.

Priorities

Nowhere in our lives is the tension greater than in the area of setting the priorities that matter most. And nothing is tougher than looking in the mirror and realizing all the mistakes we've made.

Near the end of his life, Solomon, the king of Israel and a man with power, intelligence, talents, pleasures, and riches beyond compare, put it this way in his book of Ecclesiastes:

> I observed everything going on under the sun, and really, it is all meaningless—like chasing the wind. . . . So what do people get in this life for all their hard work and anxiety? . . . "Everything is meaningless," says the Teacher, "completely meaningless!" (Ecclesiastes 1:14; 2:22; 1:2)

Too many men I have known "chase the wind," seeking fame, fortune, recognition and rewards, comfort and material things, and financial security and live lives rooted in worldly values and riches, which are "completely meaningless"—resulting in empty lives that do not satisfy. Their priorities begin there, and—since those things don't tend to leave time for anything else—they usually end there.

We have all missed too many memories and moments in our lives because of poorly ordered priorities. But it's never too late to set things straight and begin to enjoy God's blessings that are all around us. Maybe it's in the laughter of a child, or in the love we feel for our adult children, or even in the "second chance" God gives us through our grandchildren.

Making a change to a life centered on Christ, one that "chases after God," will not only help to free us from being preoccupied with our success, our careers, and our finances, but also will redirect our focus so that we can learn to embrace the priorities that truly matter.

You can begin to set the right priorities for your life through the words of Jesus: "Seek first his kingdom" (Matthew 6:33, NIV).

Take a few minutes to be quiet and spend time with God. He will lessen your worries about tomorrow and release you from the breathless pace of the world's "urgent" priorities.

Dedicating a few hours of your time to the priorities God has entrusted to you may not seem significant right now, but to those who need you, it could make all the difference in their lives—and in yours.

being versus doing

Too often, we believe that a man's value is determined solely by his achievements and measured against the standards of a world that pays homage to winning.

In our society, the struggle between *being* and *doing* starts early with our children. When we ask them what they want to be when they grow up, it really means what they want to *do*. Whatever their dreams are, they are all related to *doing*, not *being*. Those dreams tell us nothing about who our children are, or want to be, inside—what their values and priorities are—those things that will guide them through all of the things they will *do*.

Whereas men feel pressured to tie their personal value to their career, the apostle Paul stresses the importance of the fruit of the Spirit—"love, joy, peace, patience, kindness, goodness, faithfulness, gentleness, and self-control" (Galatians 5:22-23). Yet we rarely embrace these inner qualities because they don't seem to fit within the world of competitive sports and business.

Unfortunately, we end up deriving our value from what we do and what we accomplish. We confuse what we do for a living with who we are, and when what we do changes or ends, we are left trying to figure out who we are. Sadly, a staggering number of marriages end in divorce over this loss of identity and lifestyle.

Every day in my line of work, people who are completely unqualified to give performance evaluations are free to criticize my work all they like, but I don't let it negatively impact me. I decided long ago that I would analyze the criticisms from my superiors, players, assistant coaches, and even sportswriters for things that might help me improve. I know that I was created by God with all of my strengths and limitations. Somebody pointing out the limitations, real or otherwise, doesn't change my strengths or the truth that I am and will always remain a child of God.

Being versus doing—distinguishing between them will make all the difference in the lives we live.

A negative job review or getting fired can be devastating. I've been there. Though it is understandably traumatic, it doesn't have to be defining.

Whatever happens in your life, remember that your career is not you.

It should not, and does not, define who you are as a person.

DREAMS

{ It's better to have fallen

short of your dreams than

never to have tried. }

following
your dreams

I recently read an interesting article about how much Michael Westbrook, who played eight years in the NFL, *disliked* football. Despite all that he didn't like, he said that he continued to play because he was trying to please others and didn't give much thought about what pleased him.

A great deal of this book touches on relationships. Others do matter, and putting them first is often a critical part of being an uncommon man. We have a responsibility, either directly or indirectly, to shape and improve the world. But Westbrook's story illustrates an important point.

God placed certain things in your heart. He gave you gifts, abilities, dreams, and passions that no one else has. Society may not value those things as much as you do, and people may try to push you into a career that pleases their desires, but at some point, you need to answer the call that God has placed upon you and you alone. The things that excite you may not excite me, and that's great. Together we make up the tapestry of humanity and can create something beautiful.

We all have things we'd like to change about society or our world, but often we stop at complaining rather than figuring out how to change them. We need to think positively and imagine what the world would be like if we could reinvent it the way we wanted. Whether our passion is the high school graduation rate in our city or childhood diseases or homelessness, we need to think outside the box and figure out how to impact others' lives for the better.

Follow the dreams that God placed within your heart, and be prepared to face doubts. Nothing in life is easy, and we will second-guess our quest at critical times. Things change. Life throws us curveballs. Some days it feels as though we're facing blitz after blitz. People walk out of our lives and let us down. Things get confusing, loved ones misunderstand us, and relationships become tense. Fear comes and grasps us by the back of the neck, ready to carry us off and away from our dreams. And it often happens when our lives take detours that we didn't plan for, or we get pummeled by disappointments, heartaches, and tragedies.

But through all of life's challenges,
the dreams that God put in your
heart never change.

Your integrity—
your promise to yourself—
demands that you step up
and follow those dreams
to a better place, to pick
yourself up again and push on.

Follow your dreams.

BALANCE

{ Discipline is the key to

enjoying more of life the way

you want to enjoy it. }

creating balance

When I was growing up, I learned that my parents would allow me to do what I wanted to do when I disciplined myself to do what I needed to do. That is how I have also learned to allocate time to the proper priorities in my work and home life and strike a balance between the things I have to do and those I want to do. I strive to manage my time so that when the day's responsibilities are complete, I can head home.

To me, "balance" cannot be achieved simply by walking out the door at a set time or by scheduling a certain number of family activities. Rather, it is a function of our preparation and performance in those realms we are seeking to balance, measured against our prescribed priorities.

In other words, if I work hard and get my work done, I can go home knowing that I have given my employer my best. If I am diligent when I am at home about being present for Lauren and my children, I can leave with a clear conscience and right relationships when it is time to go back to the office.

The two biggest obstacles I have seen to creating balance in our lives are poor time management and workaholism. The former keeps you from ever feeling like you can allow yourself to leave the workplace, while the latter is a function of misaligned priorities, a distorted self-image, or some combination of both.

I know many men who have professional achievement as their main priority. It probably flows from a sense that this will make them more valuable as men— or at least *seem* more valuable to themselves and others. They see themselves in terms of the respect, the status, or possibly the power that they hope to achieve through the job. Still others probably have an inadequate and unfinished image of themselves, and they believe—subconsciously at times—that more work helps them to be complete.

Some men use the workplace as an escape from their families. To those I say have some guts and make some changes. Avoidance doesn't solve anything; it merely serves as a temporary salve. Go home and start restoring relationships, one day at a time.

Too many men spend too many hours at the workplace trying to fulfill the image they have created of the ideal worker.

The ability to prioritize and work through tasks during the day is the single biggest aid to having enough time to do the things you would like to do.

Doing things the right way all the time is the hallmark of a good team and the cornerstone of a balanced life.

UN COMMON MAN- HOOD

{ **choose influence over image**

In a common world, an uncommon man is aware he is a role model to someone and strives to be a good example.

RESPECT

{ **Respect others** for their

character, not status. }

respect for yourself and others

In my 1997 season with the Tampa Bucs, our team's defensive captain, a team leader, received a foolish unsportsmanlike-conduct penalty at a critical moment in a game. I was livid with him, so I brought him to the sideline and asked him what happened.

"He disrespected me," he answered. I was dumbfounded. He knew we were in the process of building a team based on poise, character, and accountability to one another. I asked him if he was willing to sacrifice the team—and our goal of winning—simply because his individual honor had been challenged or an unwritten code had been broken. His answer shocked me.

"That's all fine until somebody disrespects me." It was one of my first glimpses into this psyche of respect and disrespect and an attitude I made clear would not work for any member of our team.

A lot of people seem to believe that respect is a right, something they are entitled to upon birth. Power, position, stuff, bling—these are the sources from which too many guys think respect comes. I'm concerned that when we do show respect, we're not even respecting the things that we really should. A generation or two ago, we respected honesty, being a good provider for your family, being involved in civic organizations and church, and being a good worker in any honest occupation.

When Art Rooney Sr. was alive, as the owner of the Pittsburgh Steelers he demonstrated a lifelong caring interest in his neighborhood as well as his organization. He knew the names of the star players as well as the cleaning staff and made it clear they were all important to the success of the team. He demonstrated an authentic and sincere respect for all those whom his life touched and who touched his life.

One year, when the sanitation workers were on strike in Pittsburgh, trash was piling up everywhere around the city except in front of Art Rooney's home. As it turns out, some of the workers were picking it up on their own, because he had shown them so much respect.

Don't confuse fear with respect.

You cannot make someone respect you.

True respect starts with the way you treat others, and it is earned over a lifetime of acting with kindness, honor, and dignity.

Respect is something you earn because of your character.

Sexual Integrity

I believe that any sex outside of marriage—during or before—is wrong. You may not agree with this biblical view, but there are three basic reasons for why even sex before marriage is a bad idea—emotional, physical, and spiritual consequences.

First, because of its intimacy—or what should be its intimacy—sex can negatively impact a relationship that might otherwise have had a chance to grow into a solid friendship and possibly a marriage, which should be the goal of dating. Why sabotage the potential of this relationship or future ones for a few moments of pleasure?

Second, it often results in pregnancy and all the problems of absentee fathers. Besides, sex outside of marriage involves health risks for both partners—syphilis, gonorrhea, herpes, and HIV, to name a few. It's a terrible risk.

Third, staying sexually pure is as important for young men as women. The Bible tells us to "run from sexual sin! No other sin so clearly affects the body as this one does. For sexual immorality is a sin against your own body" (1 Corinthians 6:18). Your body is valuable. Don't be casual in what you do with it—don't give it away.

You must be vigilant with your thoughts and what goes into your mind (Matthew 6:22-23). Addiction to pornography is just as real as an addiction to alcohol or other drugs, and it can be just as damaging. Whether it creeps in through magazines, television, or the computer, the best way to avoid the addiction is to avoid the stuff altogether. Just don't go there.

Manhood is not about the number of sexual conquests you have. The idea that men are somehow to be valued for their sexual prowess has been with us for a long time. Male athletes at all levels are supposed to have a lot of women. It goes with the territory—and if you don't, people wonder what's wrong with you.

If your convictions are that you shouldn't have sex outside of marriage, you're going to face a lot of questions, sometimes even ridicule. It takes a strong man to hold up under that kind of pressure.

If you aren't yet married, focus on positive relationships grounded in friendship, and stand firm in the knowledge that you are man enough without notches in your bedpost.

It takes a strong man to be willing to follow the path of sexual purity, a much stronger man than the one who takes the easy way out and acts on what feels good at the time.

Being willing to be evaluated on a different scorecard is part of being an uncommon man.

platforms

You have multiple platforms from which to impact the world. Too often we look to others to do that, or we decide that we'll wait until later—when we have more time or money or name recognition. Or we don't think we have the expertise to change what needs to be changed and assume no one will listen to us anyway.

Not too long ago a father of a young man asked me to call his son whose fiancée had died in a car accident. The son had no idea of who I was, other than I was a guy his dad knew who had lost a son. But he knew that I cared about him, and that was enough. Was I a qualified therapist? Definitely not. But my personal grief and loss gave me a platform I would never have sought.

We all have platforms in our lives. If you're a husband, a father, a teammate, or a friend, you have a platform you can use to make a difference in the lives of those in your circle of influence. You have a chance to positively influence other people and mobilize them to change things in your community and beyond. To lift lives that need to be lifted. To make a long-term and perhaps eternal difference in those you encounter along the way.

We all have opportunities to be either "takers" or "givers." Takers receive value from the lives of others around them. We all do that, and we should, to some extent. It helps us to become all we can be. Thank God for the people I've been around who have added value to my life. But we can't just take! We also must give or add value to the lives of those around us.

You may not be a famous person, but you have a unique platform, one that can be used to impact lives that no one else can. We need to take every opportunity possible to interact with and be encouraged by other men, regardless of the setting. People respect you, believe in you, and trust you. In those cases, and others that will come, you have a platform of importance in the lives of those you touch—for their good.

Remember—you stand where no one else stands. It might be in the workplace, on the athletic field, or across the dinner table.

You may never know the impact you're having on someone who's looking up to you because of your character, your life's work, your family life, or maybe just because of your friendship.

Use your platforms wisely and in an uncommon way.

role model

We all grow up learning about life from many different sources. For better or worse, we model parents and friends, siblings and peers, and television and movie characters. I thank God for the men who built into my life—my dad, my Little League coach, my barber, my teachers, and some of the high school athletes I watched and imitated and learned from when I was ten.

That is why it's always important to see yourself as a role model. Right or wrong, somebody somewhere is watching you. I worry sometimes that as men, we take it for granted that the next generation is picking up the lessons they need for life. About 70 percent of the players who come into the NFL now don't grow up with a father in the home to help them prepare for life, and I see the difficulties they have.

Looking back, I realize that one of the added blessings of growing up with two parents was the benefit I received from the positive influence of my uncles. On weekends we would go bowling, play pinochle, go to Tigers games, and stay up to watch late-night movies. Had my father been absent, the loss of half of my relatives would have been huge.

I was able to see firsthand through my parents and their families how to treat my wife, how to relate to children, and how to treat others with respect. I learned the value of hard work and saw that *all* work was valuable and worthwhile.

We may not always see the need to be intentional about being a role model, or maybe we've become gun-shy about our shortcomings. Some guys think that because they've made so many mistakes, they can't possibly be a role model, which is definitely not true. Some of the best advice I give to young guys is, "Don't make this mistake like I did!" When I admit that I've made mistakes, I am better qualified to explain just how bad the consequences can be.

Whether you realize it or not, there are those who look up to you. Be careful of what you do and say. This is even more critical today as more and more children are growing up without a father in the home. If you and I aren't there to build into their lives, who is going to fill that void? We have to be willing to be intentional and step into their space and share in their lives and interests.

Everyone is a role model,
but not everyone is a positive
role model. So be intentional
and be a good role model.

Our kids need you.

Some of us adults need you too.

UN-
COMMON
MAN-
HOOD

{ **live your faith**

In a common world, an uncommon man strives to live his life purposefully as designed by God to have a unique and significant impact on everyone he meets.

SELF-ESTEEM

{ **You are unique, and that is**

good. That's the way God

intended it to be. }

eternal
self-esteem

So many of the issues I have discussed in this book flow from a healthy sense of self-esteem. If there were only one thing I could leave you with, it would be the understanding that you were created by God. Before you were ever born, God knew who you would be. Your abilities, interests, and passions are combined within you in a way that has never been seen before.

And God cares for you. As Jesus said, God takes care of the birds of the air and the lilies of the field, "And aren't you far more valuable to him than they are?" (Matthew 6:26). He knows your needs and desires before you even ask. He cares about you in your day-to-day living, in your excitement and in your grief, in your ups and in your downs.

I don't know what you've experienced in your life or how these experiences have made you feel about yourself, but after reading those words—that *God cares about you in every circumstance*—do you think about yourself differently? God cares about all of us—you and me.

I am concerned about kids who never come to believe that about themselves, kids who see themselves as cosmic accidents and haphazard, random events. If life is seen as accidental, then wasting my life, or taking someone else's, may not be that big of a deal. If a child feels that no one really cares about him, what do you think he begins to feel about himself?

I am troubled by a society that devalues life directly and insidiously and then markets that idea to our kids through video games, music, movies, and television. This, in turn, contributes to kids not realizing that life should be respected, nurtured, and protected. Somehow we've got to reverse this trend, and I think it starts with getting our children to see themselves as God sees them.

Life is precious and should be viewed as such. You were created by God.

You made all the delicate, inner parts of my body
and knit me together in my mother's womb.
Thank you for making me so wonderfully complex!
Your workmanship is marvelous—how well I know it.
You watched me as I was being formed in utter seclusion,
as I was woven together in the dark of the womb.
You saw me before I was born.
Every day of my life was recorded in your book.
Every moment was laid out
before a single day had passed.

Psalm 139:13-16

relationship
with Christ

God wants you to spend eternity with Him in heaven. It's pretty clear in Scripture that the way to ensure that is to recognize that you need Him. None of us is perfect, and because of our sin (falling short of God's standard for our lives), we are separated from Him. Without being holy, like God, we cannot be in a right relationship with Him—without something else occurring.

God has provided that "something else" in the person of His Son, Jesus Christ. God loved us so much that He sent His only Son to earth to die for us and take the punishment for our sinful nature, so that we could have a direct relationship with Christ and God. And all we have to do is desire to be in relationship with God, understand that we can't do it ourselves, and believe that God sent His Son for us.

It's a free gift from God.

When we believe that in our hearts and accept Jesus Christ as our Savior (He died on the cross for us) and our Lord (making Him the number one priority in our lives), we are assured of spending eternity with Him in heaven (see John 3:16-17).

Jesus often spoke of the condition of our hearts, as it reflects to the world who we are—the inner character that we display outwardly. The depth and quality of our relationship with Jesus are governed by the state of our hearts. It reveals the reasons why we do what we do. We must guard our hearts by being careful what we put into our minds. The things we dwell on will often come bubbling back up whether we want them to or not. We also must fill ourselves with God's Word by reading it. No other book will help us as much as hearing directly from God, and that's what we're doing when we read the Bible. I recommend getting a modern translation.

Prayer is simply having a heart conversation with God. Pray alone and pray with others, too, including your wife or girlfriend and your children. If you're a young person and your parents have never prayed with you—or haven't prayed with you lately—ask them to. This may feel awkward at first, but it will help bring you closer to God and closer to each other.

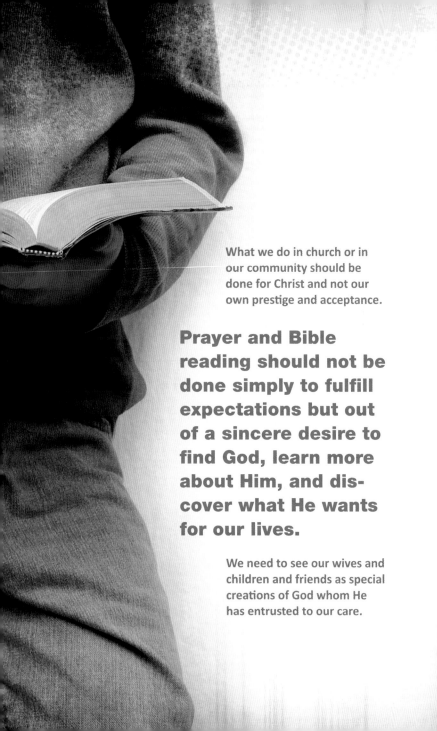

What we do in church or in our community should be done for Christ and not our own prestige and acceptance.

Prayer and Bible reading should not be done simply to fulfill expectations but out of a sincere desire to find God, learn more about Him, and discover what He wants for our lives.

We need to see our wives and children and friends as special creations of God whom He has entrusted to our care.

faith

We don't control everything. That's difficult for us to admit sometimes, but I think that's central to some of the issues that plague us as men. Our best efforts to control the world will always fall short.

Therefore, I am summoning faith all the time: Faith that the pilot of the flight I'm on won't fall asleep and that whoever programmed the traffic signals set the other side to red when mine goes green. Faith that my children will come home safely when the school day is over.

Quarterbacks throw most of their passes to a set spot believing the receiver will run to that spot. The receiver runs his precise route believing the ball will be at that spot. Defensive players must "trust the system" and stay in their assignments rather than instinctively running to the ball.

We can act as though we're in control of life, or that we've got things figured out, but Jesus was clear that we are not promised tomorrow. Only God knows how everything will play out. And our lives will be more effective if we live according to His game plan rather than trying to take matters into our own hands.

Paul wrote in his letter to the Romans that "in all things God works for the good of those who love him" (Romans 8:28, NIV). This doesn't mean that everything will work out the way we hope, but that God has everything in His sights, and that He will cause everything to work together for *His* purpose. In *His* time. Our problems, our worries, our sins, and our pain will work together in God's time and for God's purpose.

And that is where faith comes in. Some things are beyond our comprehension. Some days—or years—it seems as if nothing goes right. Our teenage children behave in ways that worry us, and our marriages may be going through a desert, where things just aren't what they should be. Our coaches, our teachers, our parents, or our bosses may be acting unreasonably or treating us unfairly.

Even in the face of all those circumstances, God is there. God is with us every step of the way, and He knows where this is all headed.

I know I can't make it through life relying solely on my own smarts and strength. Life is too tough, and too many things come up that I have no control over.

Don't try to fool yourself into thinking that self-reliance is possible. It is foolish to think we don't have to have faith in anyone else. It's also a lonely way to go through life.

And it leaves out the perspective of eternal life.

purpose

So why are you here, anyway?

I believe that God gave you the passions and gifts that you have and the platform that only you enjoy. I believe that the imprint you are meant to leave on this world is not accidental or coincidental. Your life has been intentionally designed by God to have a uniquely significant and eternal impact on the world around you, everyone you meet, and many you may never meet.

Think about that for a moment. What if we all lived our lives embracing that idea as true? What would we attempt to do, and what difference would we make in the lives of those around us? What problems in the world might get solved that we never would have attempted otherwise? What would our communities and schools look like? How many of our children and youth would find hope for tomorrow?

Though I do think there are things that each of us can do to improve ourselves, I believe first and foremost that I operate from God's grace. That grace is not a license to do whatever I choose but rather an understanding that despite my best efforts, I will fall short in my striving for God, and that's okay. When it happens, I just get up and press on toward the mark.

And as I press on, I think that I am called to ask, "What kind of world do I want?" Anyone can complain, but I need to be prepared to offer thoughts on how I can improve—myself, my home, my town, my nation, and the world.

We have all seen people less fortunate than ourselves, others who seem to have little hope for anything to change in their lives without some external intervention. We may not have the full solution or the wherewithal to solve these problems ourselves—but we do have our own passions and abilities, and we can begin to make a difference today.

I believe my purpose is this: to serve the Lord and use all that He has given me to help others to the best of my ability. When I'm staying focused on that, it allows me to find the joy and abundant life that Christ promised, even if we don't win the Super Bowl or I don't meet every goal that I have for my life.

You're not always going to reach those things you really desire; in fact, failure may happen more often than not.

But you can find peace and happiness in the knowledge that you're striving within your real purpose that honors God.

If you're striving only for yourself, you'll be dissatisfied, always yearning for more, while the world waits.

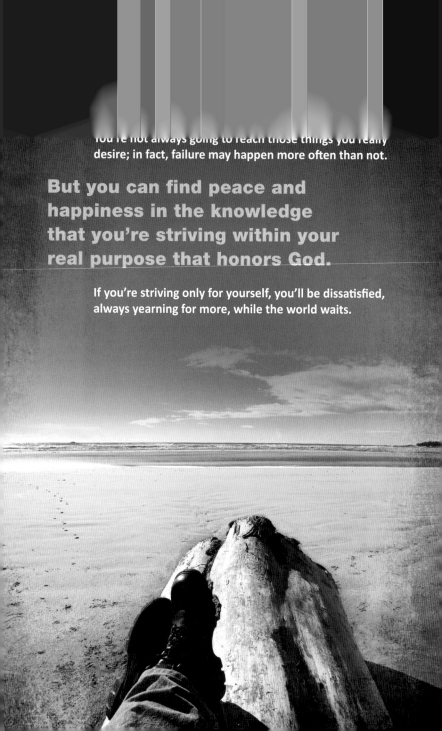

significance

It's easy to fall into the trap of thinking that a CEO, or a celebrity, or a billionaire is significant. Those people might have significance, but it's not simply because of their position or resources. Significance is a much deeper issue than that.

Have you figured out what God has placed you here to do, and are you doing it to the best of your abilities? Therein lies the answer to significance.

It's a liberating place to be once you figure it out. I was fortunate enough to coach a team to a Super Bowl win, but it never was an all-encompassing quest for me. I realized that winning it was not going to make my life complete and not winning it certainly wouldn't ruin my life. Instead, I tried to focus at each step along the way on those priorities I had already decided were important: being a good coach, learning enough to become a better one, and spending my free time with my family and in ministry opportunities.

I wanted to win. God wired me to be competitive, probably you as well. However, the best measuring stick of that competitive nature is whether we are true to the call in our hearts and act on that call to the best of our abilities.

Your life is not a series of accidents and coincidences. God knew before you were born that you would be where you are today, would have the influence over those whom you do, as well as those you will impact down the line. Through it all, the legacy you leave on this earth will determine what your life on earth meant.

God calls us to be faithful, not necessarily successful. He calls us to follow those dreams that are in our hearts and to pursue them with all our might. Sometimes they will proceed in ways that make them a "success" in worldly terms, but other times it may feel more like futility. Sometimes we'll be able to witness changed lives, and sometimes the only life we can see changed is our own.

God's scorecard is different from ours. He does want to bless us, but His scorecard doesn't use money or material possessions or fame or status. He judges by the state of our hearts and our desire to serve Him.

"The Lord doesn't see things the way
you see them. People judge by outward appearance,
but the Lord looks at the heart" (1 Samuel 16:7).

Don't ever sell yourself short. God's purposes are greater than man's purposes. There is much to do and much that you are capable of doing.

What kind of world do you want?
Think anything. Just be careful what you wish for.
Start now to be uncommon.

Also from Tony Dungy and Tyndale House Publishers

Quiet Strength

Uncommon

The Mentor Leader

The One Year Uncommon Life Daily Challenge

Tony Dungy on Winning with Quiet Strength (DVD)

Dare to Be Uncommon: A 4-Week Curriculum Character-Building Challenge (DVD)

Playbook for an Uncommon Life (6-pack)